Regulator

Regulator

Benjamin Dodds

PUNCHER & WATTMANN

© Benjamin Dodds 2014

This book is copyright. Apart from any fair dealing for the purposes of study and research, criticism, review or as otherwise permitted under the Copyright Act, no part may be reproduced by any process without written permission. Inquiries should be made to the publisher.

First published in 2014
Published by Puncher and Wattmann
PO Box 441
Glebe NSW 2037
http://www.puncherandwattmann.com
puncherandwattmann@bigpond.com

National Library of Australia
Cataloguing-in-Publication entry:

Dodds, Benjamin
Regulator

ISBN 9781922186478

I. Title.

A821.3
Cover design by Matthew Holt

Printed by McPhersons Printing Group

This project has been assisted by the Australian Government through the Australia Council, its arts funding and advisory body.

Contents

1. *Regulator*

Thinning our little herd	9
Weed	10
Our Lady of Yanco	11
Wyndham's Crow	12
Idol	13
Regulator	14
yanco road	16
Touchstone	17
One Summer	18
Pig	19
A kind of Christmas came	20
Cringe	22
Easter Parade	24

2. *Human Awe*

"In telepathy, space doesn't matter"	27
Forty Years — 2009	28
Others	29
Two Books	30
Unravelled	32
clean air and wide open spaces	34
Sometimes	35
Theirs	36
Unsheathed	38
Under Cicadas	39

Emptying Out	40
After a quoll	41
Magnapinna species	42
homoeostasis	44
Host	45
The Challicum Bunyip	46
Stranger Danger	48

3. *There's No Putting Them Out*

Man at Home	51
Things Fall Apart	52
Remnant	53
Observer	54
Novel	56
How many times	57
starstudded	58
Captive	59
The spiders are here	60
Struggle Street	61

4. *Perfectly Normal Sons*

Wrested	65
satisfaction	66
tower poem	67
München	68
Subcutaneous	69
Prodigal Son (and his partner)	70

1.

Regulator

Thinning our little herd

For weeks
we had Baskerville
hounds in our heads
sweeping bold arcs
through feathered darkness
at the porch light's circle edge.
My father's too-long absence
and the distortion
of farm-night acoustics
surely exaggerated their size
but the rigid carnage we'd find
stitched to the morning's frozen
grass did little to lessen unease.
A man who was not our father
barked stark instruction
at my brother and me:
foolproof steps
for burning a gutted calf.

Weed

Since it slipped unobserved
past his curlicued garden gate
Mr Paterson has had a lot to answer for.
Its copper bloats and kills the cows
but its nectar saved the apiarists
who called it *Salvation Jane*.
Every twirling knifeful
tastes and smells
of the perpetual weed
that shoves aside anything
you might want to grow
in a newly graded paddock
and plants its purple self instead.
No child watered by the veins
of the turbid Murrumbidgee
can frame a summer memory
without border curls of
Riverina Bluebell
creeping in at the sides—
a bristling Art Nouveau.

Our Lady of Yanco

Mary
rendered in concrete
stands serenely in a block of the same stuff
inside the sheltering niche of an upended bathtub.
She was built to last— her salmon drapery
applied over two consecutive weekends
to ensure the undercoat dried completely
before the laying-on of her blue
in All Weather Exterior.
She's faded only slightly since then—
mostly in the face.
Who could be blamed
for closing their eyes
to the rippling convection
of such Summer sun?

Wyndham's Crow

A passage in *The Day of the Triffids*
gives us a field of blinded sheep
butting and breaking themselves
against harsh fences. Immediately
I'm back at the Fisher place
where Benji and I would march
across clovered grazing paddocks
gloriously filling in days of time.
A lamb we'd passed early one morning
now staggered like a drunk
as a blue-black crow
perched on its woollen skull
and drew out strings of elastic
gore from almost-empty sockets.
In Wyndham's book
the bird would also be blind
but even so
I imagine it would still find
the feeble thing and unfasten
its redundant eyes
by feel.

Idol

His older brother leans
against the breakfast bar

dangling lure at hips
sectioned rod in hand

and proudly disgorges the events
of his *Boy's Own* weekend

with the kids from Cudgel Creek.
Drum nets set in the middle of the river

tentpoles upset in the middle of the night.
Captivated heads on hands

propped atop the granite bench
we chew on discs of dried banana.

Regulator

Galvanised gates
lift to divide the calm
from the chaotic:
input—process—output.
On this narrow bridge
the world is out of whack.
It's like listening to a stereo
with the sound wound up
and the balance knob
turned fully left or right.

      On the bank
a fading slump of a sign
shows a black stick-figure
in the throes of the Australian Crawl
overlaid with a thick circle
bisected by an equally thick
diagonal line.
Metres from here
dangerously adolescent men
in wet sucking board-shorts
queue at the bridge to drop again
into the irrigation canal.

The sleeping surface
snares their bombs and pin-drops
from the baking sky
and drags them down
where it's gut-punch cold.
Chased by churning echoes
they become a function of
the violent process of current.

To funnel through its breathless
grip takes maybe ten seconds
      long enough to induce
a personal panic
which must be neatly filed away
before the final re-emergence
into tingling spume and
the muted whoops of brotherhood
back at the regulator
shockingly far upstream.

On Monday's school
bus they lift thin senior shirts
over awkward shoulders
to compare backs broad
and brown as hens'
eggs lacerated by steel
from neck to crack.

yanco road

don't touch she said   so i didn't.
we knelt over the bird in the dust
eyes open to a world crowded with ants.
it was a galah   common as anything
thousands of them screamed above us
and chewed the eucalypt tops
to dead fingers raking the sky.

we watched one scramble
through scattered bark-ribbon
not far from where we stood. it
bobbed and swayed but faltered
through fear of our intent.
afraid to come closer yet quite riskily near
it danced a stupid arc in the darkening dusk.

she took my hand and we left the feathered mess
but i trailed to watch the bird nudge its partner.
after a silence she told how they pair for life
that these pink and grey things keep companions and i
thought of the ants and the nodding sad mate
as it rocked alone by the side of the road
and began to feel for the loss of a friend

even though it was not one of mine.

Touchstone

My father once came home
after a month of working away
with a wedge of chipped basalt
in his lumpy sports bag.
The leathery impression
of a single slender leaf
ran from one sharp edge
to another.
This was the hour
when *fossil*
was petrified
in my still-plastic brain.
It became my holotype
and reinforced itself quietly
each time I stood
at the dressing table.
Even now
I feel the smoothness
of storm-coloured stone
when I read
or hear the word.
I reckon he knew
exactly what he was doing
when he handed me that imprint
but it's not the sort of thing you
confirm with a crane-driver dad
is it?

One Summer

When viewing events
through the dismantled biro barrel
that's childhood's grasp of things
it seemed disproportionately rash
that my mother would close (for good)
the Yanco Village Tearooms and Ice Cream
Parlour in the middle of a weekday morning
just because the couple that
owned the town's other store refused
to sell me five loaves of bread.

Pig

There's a pig in the grass
and broken bricks
and caked pads of sawdust
piled up behind the gun club's rifle range.
It's only slightly buried beneath it all.

The punk-rock haircut, subversive green,
is healthier than any lawn in town.
The white smiling teeth
(top set only— the lower lies in soil)
could sell Colgate on TV.

After its rest, it'll
stand and shake the
turf and building rubble
from its lightly downed back,
then prance down the mound
on pretty, pointed trotters,

or so I tell my nephew
who reaches to prod
the balloon of belly
with a bent,

spent welding rod.

A kind of Christmas came

to what we generously called
our station
one hot December day.

The school was dragged
down to the wheat silos
on the train line

to see a single engine pull up
royal blue
sounding far too forceful

without its thirty cars
of grain in tow.
The place was one we knew

not from catching trains
(you couldn't do that anymore)
but through playing out of bounds

on endless Escher ladders
and crawling over catwalks
to high gantry stages

that held us over mountains
of suffocating grain.
The kid whose parents ran the pool

found a detonator
in the State Rail storehouse
across the tracks

and took off four fingers at the hilt.
And now the weekday town was here
or all its kids at least.

Using a cotton wool beard
to wipe his greasy brow
a lanky sweat-stained man

in poorly-fitting felt
stepped down from the cabin
to the sun-cracked platform slab

and issued us packets of Twisties
NOT FOR INDIVIDUAL SALE
emblazoned across their backs.

Cringe

If these ruins were Pompay Springs,
somewhere in the southern shadow
of a now-dormant Mt. Versuvy
in the Central West Slopes and Plains
of New South Wales,
you'd pay your ten bucks
for Jodie
(descendant
of two scorched survivors)
to walk you past
the recreated bora rings
and paraphrase the plaques
screwed to petrified canoe trees.

Think brown-painted shop dummies,
loin-clothed and propped up
outside shaggy replica humpies—
an attempt to *bring history to life*.
Before being shown out,
you'd pick up a plastic refracting-ruler
for the neighbour's kid
feeding the dogs back home
and head off
to refill your travel mug
at some declining servo,
never having been trusted
to step into any roped-off areas.

But here in the Bay of Naples,
in the absence of Pompeiian Jodies
and *Non Toccare* signs,
I stand alone, cloistered
in an asphyxiated family's home.
When I reach and touch
the slaggy wall, because I can,
a sizable piece of millennial guilt
drops between my
sensible walking shoes.

Easter Parade

A spring-loaded gorilla
stalks up and down an unlidded cage,
climbs the sides and lobs tins of peaches
over the bars at my cross-legged parents
and me.
They fall all around us, Letona-labelled.
One bites a clean
moon in the earth with its edge.
I avoid the eyes behind the eyes as he passes
yet wonder which father or uncle's inside.
The cage is the wood-carter's trailer,
the ill-fitting fur has hung
across the road in that window for years,
but Dad can't make me take this can.

2.

Human Awe

"In telepathy, space doesn't matter"

Edgar Mitchell, Apollo 14 Astronaut

he is one of three men in a metal tube
hurtling away at a speed so great

its meaning shorts and fails.
reality spins jettisoned in their airless wake.

inside banal procedure: diagnostics
and cycled periods of rest.

it's his turn now.
the tightly elasticised hammock

allows a type of gravity.
he knows it's a lie but his overtaxed body

grants the benefit of the doubt.
sleep will pour in after one last task.

it's the ideal test to conduct
in stealth   no apparatus necessary

nothing but a crowded card of numbers
and six minutes of continuous thought.

in a quiet house a group gathers
around a kitchen table. one will be the scribe.

Forty Years — 2009

I've always been achingly jealous
that my parents watched
as it really happened out there.
I buy all the books
        have witnessed the moment
        more times than I can count
yet can never say in truth
that I sat cross-legged
on government-grey carpet
while everybody
        even the jaded teachers
felt down here a pull
from another place
        an ossified landscape
that hadn't been real
until two men
inserted themselves
silently into it.

Others

Will they appear silently
on our horizon's doorstep

heralding their sudden arrival
with flashes of Alessi chrome

or send word in advance
from across gulfs of time

a message to fold out the sofa
for envoys not yet conceived

at the time of transmission?
Perhaps they'll simply pass us by

indifferent in sleek behemoths
on the way to a place less

parochial than here. Of what
real interest is a floating

termite-mound to possibly
non-corporeal entities? Human

awe has always aimed skyward.
Unfocussed waves

radiate from organic transmitters
waiting for a wave back.

Two Books

If a sudden strange amnesia
were to befall us all
and a fresh new generation
      true tabula rasa children
      sired of ultimate innocence
were to rise
they would laugh
and shake their bell-clear heads
to read dusty tales of risen corpses
and disproportionate paternal
anger over stolen fruit.

And down the years
when one of them unsure
took up an old book
from which he began to glean a trust
in the idea of a lonely being
      who created man
      exactly as he still appeared
      who drowned all but two
      of every kind
      and still monitored silently
      keeping daily scores for all
the others would set this person down
and hand him another book—
one not yet written when
our own antecedents
first entertained such ideas.

Therein he would find
unshakeable solace
in the knowledge that
of all possible permutations
of individual life
his own came about
when uncountable others did not.
Seek awe in that
and he need never seek it
elsewhere again.

Unravelled

Never referred to explicitly
electrophoresis gels feature
alongside anonymous lab technicians

safety-goggled henchmen
wielding delicate glass pipettes
and endless arrays of plastic phials

in footage furnishing 30-second
news pieces about genetics
and 'ethically troubling' breakthroughs.

Throw in the phrase *playing God*
and you're there.
'Running gels' means

laying out ladders of striated DNA
that fade into chemical whispers
and ghost down the page.

To unfurl protein's coils
you'll need a solution of Acrylamide
our dreaded antagonist

and known neurotoxin.
Acrylamide even looks dangerous
with its cross-braced capital A

dangerous enough to knock me
off my feet after a long and hot bath

on a departmental flex day

to find myself naked and dry
on the bedroom floor
involuntarily trawling

the bridge of my nose
up and down beige carpet
in a wide red arc.

I've since read
Acrylamide accrues
in the system.

That ground-in stain
with its rusting brightness
smiles up at me still.

clean air and wide open spaces

it starts with softly muttered awe
striding into cicada-throbbing bush
farther and farther from the car

after the quickening trek
when the notebook and colours
are put away unused

the whispering enormity of gorge
or valley or plummeting cliff
becomes an increasing concern

look for that guard rail
     the dribbly splash
     of hand-painted demarcation

some sign that   though you're out alone
this place is no stranger to people
who might round that bend as you stare

     but their absence breeds dread.
this is when the swarming eucalypts
and gaping sky work in tandem

to chant inside your head
they crowd you out
     because one man swimming

in so much space
poses no challenge
to a host of screaming trees

Sometimes

at 3 in the morning
there's nothing I wouldn't give
to see an ovoid capsule
settle with an almost inaudible thrum
on Downstairs Lisa's immaculately kept lawn
just below the bedroom window
of my first storey Petersham flat.
When in that mood
I'd even accept
the half-snatched flickering-out
of my private patch of stars
that might have been caused
by the magnetic swell
and silent passing of something
sleek and immense across the sky.
Always though
it's spoilsport reason
that threads the nothing-filled night
with my sleep.

Theirs

This country has no true shrike.
We have birds of similar appearance

shrike-like species in plumage and size
      the shrike-tit the cuckoo-shrike

but none can claim
the pure unhyphenated name.

      I want to own this bird as I could
(should I wish) the galah

      want to have the way
it impales its prey

on thirsty acacia spines
      to see it concentrate

its meagre weight
and drive down arcing bodies

of lizards   moths and frogs
      an action of foresight

assuring a curved beak
an easy future meal.

      Show me the browsing giraffe
that shares its eye-line

with the skewered corpse of a mouse.
    I envy the African poets

who know the call
of the only predatory songbird.

Unsheathed

Split up the back like dirty
slips, the ghostly cases
stand unmoving in the heat.
They mark the places from which
these prawn-eyed death-rattlers
have lifted themselves
on broad leadlight blades into
summer's ripening dryness.

A far-off version of
me holds one up close,
Yorick-style.
The alien skin balances on
up-turned palm, primed
to catch even the
slightest breath of breeze.
It's hard not to wonder
just how it might feel
to peel oneself
from within a congealing shroud,
to leave a pair of crystal domes
where obsidian eyes
once nested
                unblinking.

Under Cicadas

like the electronic creations
of a straight-to-video madman

the black things throw off
rays of thrumming heat

summer's burning breath
I think it's of their making

convection-waves
radiate unceasingly

from sun-hardened abdomens
tightly bound up

the size of a house mouse
these black princes

positioned equidistant
sense the proximity of neighbours

and adjust output accordingly
constant calibration is necessary

to keep this hell
stable

Emptying Out

The slippage is what has really lingered:
the sloughing-off of grey-pelted skin
and thicker sheets of liquid muscle
beneath   then the way it all ran
through the floor of that cage
when two boys lifted it out
of the water— an open hammock
of chicken wire supporting
the thousand-sluiced frame
of a fellow live-born vertebrate
as all else sifted through.
Set for yabbies the summer before
this forgotten net   drift-shifted
had penned a sleek rat and laid out
for one of us an undeniable homology
that triggered a spill of devon
and white bread—
the sickness of mammalian decay.

After a quoll

Outside the tent
this morning
on dew-wet grass:
the hollowed carapace
of a crayfish
whose faintly red lining
brought passionfruit leather
to mind.

Magnapinna species

The elbowed thing drifts
and darts   drifts and darts

trailing a metres-long train of tendrils:
Rapunzel as incubus.

Held tenuously in bilious floodlight
it hangs in relief against

the darkness of this Vernian depth.
The remotely controlled camera

jerks on clumsy x-y axis
to keep it in frame.

At once this pudendal creature
transfixes and utterly repels.

Without instruction
the muscles at my core

brace when it's on screen.
She erupts into the room

one dangling earring already hung
the other in search of a hole

tilts her head
and in jarring tones

demands an opinion on how she looks.
She lobs another question over the shoulder

on her way out   not staying to see
me catch the bouquet or if it's caught at all.

Is that in space or the sea?

homoeostasis

slowly, slowly   *lentamente*
the density of water lessens
and that of air increases

nobody notices this but me

only genius machines
with glacial ticking patience
can detect the change
from thick to thin and vice versa

nobody sets them to check

on the day of equilibrium
our larger lungs
grown in measured secrecy
in the earth of our chests
will share the briny air
with futurefish
as tidewinds bear up
kites with hook-strung tails
reeled out by
ever-enterprising boys

Host

The encrusted
growth at the top of
my shin is the shape
of a bivalve's convex shell.
From a tiny puncture at its lower
edge, a slender black extension
emerges and then retracts,
barbed at intervals
like an insect's leg.
The one who steps in, I presume,
is my father. *Like
a Band-Aid*, he warns,
and drags back
a strip of the scab
to reveal the movement of
something large and undeniably
insectoid. The glossy hornet,
banded black and yellow,
would pass for a plastic one,
but for its rhythmic twists
and the stinging panic it
plants in my now-open
wound. Reaching in
and pinching behind its head,
he looks off to one side,
stays his breath,
and it's out,
trailing a couple of wings
still wetly connected
by strands of anaemic flesh.

The Challicum Bunyip

They drag it out of Fiery Creek
in the cool of the mountain's shadow
and drop it heavily
onto the bank.
The gritty slush sounds like the sea.

The head hangs pendulously
down its side,
rests against rigid spears
whose fire-hardened roots
bite slime-slicked fur and flesh.

The thrashing tail has died
into the limp handhold
by which it's hauled
up into swaying grasses.
Naked silhouettes stand by.

Tall ones shelter short ones,
shining eyes and teeth
between their knees.
Here is a thing to be seen.
Here is a thing to remember.

The tallest, with skin of polished night,
kneels like a newly made hinge
and with a single slash
of something dark and dense
brings forth what lies inside.

The hard and soft remains of child
spill out with a steaming sigh,
draped about with reed-ribbon,
algae-furred mussels
and feathers from bathing birds.

The men and their boys
outline the vast thing
with a tall fence of spears
before avoiding the place
for a full seasons' cycle.

They'll return to clear
the then-empty shape
by removing its turf like a hide,
and lead daisy-chains of short ones
to stand within its bounds.

In another time, men filling up maps
will label this land Victoria
after a woman they've never seen,
and the mountain Ararat
after the setting of an apocryphal tale.

Remarking upon a strange fading form
etched at the edge of a piddling creek,
some will look to the strange fading People
who skirt the edges of burgeoning towns,
figures too faint to be traced.

Stranger Danger

Banksia cones part tribesman lips
to breathe their unheard chorus.

Far too many mouths sprout
at Fibonacci intervals

through brittle pubic bush.
A grip and a twist is what it takes

to dislodge one from its woody place,
the same procedure

Gibbs's miscreants must workshop
and self-administer

before descending
in curmudgeonly packs

on long, barbed, barefoot limbs
to stalk sap-juicy gumnuts—

green-capped homunculi
with ruddy-cheeked bums.

They'd drive white panel vans
if they could.

3.

There's No Putting Them Out

Man at Home

It's too easy
to place the frozen crown
of a broken glass
amidst the nest of detritus
that half-fills the kitchen bin.
Easier at least
than to wrap and roll it
in cushioning newsprint
the way my mother taught me.
There's prudence too
in placing the eager edge
of a can's excised lid
inside the empty thing itself
instead of the way I've dropped it
keen curve up
beside the jagged glass.
And later today
there's the very real chance
that I'll pivot my weight in
to break down the bulk
and open up space
for consequent castaways
only to slice wide
the face of my palm
despite a daylong mantra of caution.

Things Fall Apart

Waking to find a complete set of teeth
all present and accounted for
is a singular sort of relief
that can only follow from those slow dreams
in which the breakability of manmade things
migrates to man himself.
When trapped unwaking,
it's not only possible for incisors
to be unpegged and drawn out
by the white matrix of an apple's flesh,
but also for nails to lift and come away
as gifts to the wind
when scratching a decent itch.
Still, how reliable is daytime solidity?
Best not to test the stresses
of nature's dovetails, fastenings and pins
lest they prove as fallible as I privately fear.

Remnant

My hands won't stop smelling of onion—
it repulses and fixates.
Again and again
I raise them to my face
to monitor the immovable scent
that's been with me
    a part of me
since dinner on Tuesday.
Awareness of my own porosity
keeps me awake.
What other essences
    benignly odourless or otherwise
do I take in
unconsenting
through this skin?
It's the recess phone call home again
    then being bundled away retching
after yielding to the compulsion to touch
the glass thermometer
above the bag and coat hooks
    filled   as I'd been told
with creeping silver poison.

Observer

On the 445 from Balmain,
in situ, second from the tail,
I'm unmoving as Dian Fossey
in a netting-draped hide
(like the one she never used):
dangerous young men
etch signatures, or derivations thereof,
into sheets of Pilkington glass.
Powered by a battery of energy drinks,
they leap from the seat behind me
to those across the aisle, then again.

Choosing to be aloof
and forward-facing, folding away
Teacher, Concerned Citizen, I do nothing
say nothing
see nothing
until two or three stops
past the ambulance station
where, with tattooed arcs of armspan,
they measure their way to the rear
door and out and away.

With a headshake
intended for the reassurance of others,
I turn to examine the upholstered scene:
the castings of glossy black cans,
the dust of ground glass.
Clive James asks where bus
vandals get their diamond pens.
These gripped razor blades dextrously

between thumb and forefinger.

Novel

The man across from me
is mouthing *The Lord of the Rings*.
The second part, to be precise.

Such uttering is commonplace
in young classrooms, or in the pews
of a quiet church, but here

it's exotic enough to ensure
my own book hangs closed around a finger
while his lips whisper at speed,

impervious to the snagging bramble
of almost impossible consonant clusters
strewn before him in Departure Lounge 22.

How many times

have I stayed my flying fingers
above the lettered keys

to hang in pause and hope
to catch the tiny sound again?

Soft, yet so specific and precise;
a miniature abacus clack

that comes when I'm alone,
when the rooms are pressingly still

and the only movement is with me.
But I have found the source now,

caught it in the act, and remembered
that I am not alone

when no one's home.
He's become an object,

not inanimate, I'll admit,
but a pretty extension of the sideboard,

all shuddering fins and tail, as he
turns tiny stones in his lenticular cell.

starstudded

beneath our radiant southern cross
cumcharged boys bow down
to have its sawtoothed kitepoints etched
in greenveined permastain
across the spread of suncured shoulders
over the tensile arcs of calves
and under tightly puckered navels

the fistful of suns
stellar swastika
looks down   looses a flood
of sickly light
makes strangers coldly stranger
keeps the coast clear

on weekday mornings
a keen and patient eye
might catch the constellation
albeit dim
setting behind
the crisp horizon
of a dry cleaned collar

Captive

Amid tour guidance
(Flemington, the MCG)
and the shorthand speak of old friends,
one of the pets they'd just picked up from
a stay at the cattery
pissed and shat itself
in the back of their Yaris.
During the letting-out of all it had held in
for two days of deaf and unresponsive silence,
it skewered me, fellow backseat passenger,
with steady sulphurous eyes.
Bell and collar tamed nothing;
what was in that box
was wild, alive and rigid with hate.

The spiders are here

Last night, a sprawled grey one
planted its hugeness by the front door.
The wet outburst of its kernelled abdomen
was necessary. Once they're in,
there's no putting them out.

And today, the black economy
of a furled umbrella nestled itself in miniature
beneath the latch of the garden gate.
A creased bank statement made a neat streak of it.

Vigilance
or soon the swaying needle-rise
and drawbridge-drop of two leading legs
mount the mattress summit
to plant nightmare's waking flag.

Struggle Street

A pitbull pup launched
through the void of a screenless
second-storey window breaks
four legs and siphons
from readers a soup
of tears and muttered tutting.

These toothless/heartless owners
should be licensed. Where do they find the cash
to buy their Crayola cartons of Horizon 50s anyway?

4.

Perfectly Normal Sons

Wrested

Splayed out like Vitruvian boys
on the concrete cap

of the raised water tank
they draw a day of hoarded heat

through buttocks and backs.
The rude familiar honk of an approaching car

and a wholesome *hello* launched
through the kitchen window below

shatter their world completely.
Screaming drifts of galahs

pink and grey as the sky that holds them
signal the death of this hot-blooded day.

One last protracted clasp of hands
and two monkeys skim

down the parchment-smooth skin of a
convenient branch.

On the anaemic lawn   two country
mothers smile over a quick

cup of tea at the reluctant arrival
of perfectly normal sons.

satisfaction

holding taut barbed-wire with one hand
and myself with the other
I gaze at the ground
as hundreds of shining grey dust droplets
roll away from the rotting fence post
down the hill
moving like mercury.
The drumming piss
makes surf of the dirt
churns it into frothy mud.
Apostle birds (perhaps twelve of them)
launch and fan off above my head
upset as I shake off the last bead
and refasten.

Tower Poem

Our water tower had battlements
art deco moulding around the rim

that earned it a heritage listing
and constant debate amongst the kids

in town who'd heard it was really
bone dry and that if refilled you'd

hear the powdery slap of collapse
all the way out to Wamoon.

We flattened ourselves against its cool
on the way to senior sport.

the same cool that ran through
the ranging shadow in which

a station wagon pulled up and presented
a ride to the river

with a man in oil-stained overalls.
I said I wouldn't go but stayed

through the crisp snap of three press-studs.
I'd never seen or been that hard.

München

Sharp red wine in a half-sized bottle
mincing men with middle-aged stomachs
distended like dead cattle.
Through moustaches
      grotesque
      Daliesque
they speak to me about the cold.
From his corner wall-bracket
the weatherman forecasts snow.
I tell them I've never seen it before
part polite conversation
part lie
and rest my gaze
on a row of paunches
too late to avoid the image
of fleshy countersunk penises.
I ask a huge man
how often he uses his English.
He lisps something
about a private lesson
later that night in his room.
They all hoot at this attempt at
coquetry. Just enough perverted
vanity and the knowledge
that Sydney is so far away
ratchet my mouth to a smile.
The next morning
I skid like Bambi did in the
wrong sort of shoes for snow.

Subcutaneous

since it happened
I have been waiting
for this other event

for a blood-crust to form
for the thin weeping to slow
and for you to move within me

I have seen it in my head
your white fingers fumble
with curve-pointed scissors

as you slip one blade under
and snip the thread at a point
beside the precise black knot

I feel a sudden slackening
just beneath the surface of my flesh
and the anticipated slide

of scrupulous slicing nylon
at a depth whose nerves lie dormant
all times but this

I sit ready tonight
and see you sense a mood in me
incongruous to you

Prodigal Son (and his partner)

A city boyfriend
when taken to stay with parents
in rural Queensland
must be made to feel
that it's normal and neighbourly
to step in and out
of nearby paddocks at will.
It's customary to laugh
at his ignorance of barbed wire
and the methods of rendering it benign
by lifting or lowering its strands.
Looping a gate's galvanised chain
back upon itself and over
the mushroomed stay
must be done whilst speaking of
something entirely unrelated,
such should appear the second nature
of gate administration
in a boy born and bred on the land.
After the well-timed peach of sunset is
photographed and declared to be gorgeous,
the homeward path should take in views
of whomever's herd. And when they stamp,
lower horned heads and begin to follow,
smile knowingly at his sweet
unease—they're only cows—
whilst shepherding him over the fence
by the most direct route possible.

Acknowledgements

A significant number of these poems first appeared in literary journals and on poetry websites and blogs. Many thanks go to the editors of these publications for supporting my work and that of other new poets: *Cordite Poetry Review, Southerly, AustralianReader.com, Etchings, Harvest, dotdotdash, kipple, Mascara Literary Review, ChickenPinata. com, Bluepepper, Blue Dog, Earthly Matters: Biology and Geology Poems, Page Seventeen, Famous Reporter, Australian Poetry Members' Anthology 2012* and *Australian Poetry Collaboration*.

Not nearly enough gratitude can go to David Musgrave, Dani Corliss, Stuart 'SBS' Barnes, Rhyll McMaster, Tricia Dearborn and Norm Neill and his brilliant Wednesday Night Poetry crowd for their invaluable feedback and suggestions throughout Regulator's various forms.

Extra thanks to Laura Matarese, Lauren Nagel, Kristie Naimo and 'Scary' Helen Keenan for their supreme friendship and support over the many years I've known them. Thanks also to Viv and Gail— mistresses of flattery.

Finally, all the love in the world goes to Helen, Don, Toby, Claire and Hannah Dodds and my wonderful Carlo Caponecchia.

www.ingramcontent.com/pod-product-compliance
Lightning Source LLC
Chambersburg PA
CBHW030813090426
42737CB00010B/1255